Becoming Sherlock

The Power of Observation and Deduction

STEFAN CAIN

DEDICATION

To all those who strive to see that which others cannot, in an effort
to become happier and more successful in life.

"The world is full of obvious things which nobody by any chance ever observes."

–Sherlock Holmes

ACKNOWLEDGEMENTS

As you read this book, you'll want to remember the fictional character, Sherlock Holmes, and recognize the impact this character played on future generations of all ages.

Contents

1 Sherlock's Brain-Attic   1

2 The Ultimate Power of the Senses to Deduct and Induce   5

3 Sherlock's Deductive & Inductive Method   17

4 Increasing Your Powers of Observation   35

5 Taking Notes to Improve Attentiveness   39

6 Creativity and Imagination in Problem-Solving   45

7 Improving Your Memory Skills   57

8 Making Deductions from Body Language & Detecting Deceit   65

9 How to Improve Your Deductive & Inductive Skills   76

10 How to Improve Your Decision-Making Ability through Deduction   83

Conclusion   89

INTRODUCTION

Wouldn't you love to have "superhuman" observational and deductive abilities like Sherlock Holmes? Well, contrary to popular belief, the capability to observe and deduce is not a natural ability. Professional detectives actually take years of practice to cultivate good habits of observation. This book is a shortcut.

You might think that you're not an observant person or you just don't have that ability. Well, you do! The truth is that you have *subconsciously chosen* not to see the details in the world around you. So, all you have to do is make a **choice** to want to become more aware… and watch how it will change your life!

- Do you want to impress others with your newfound ability to analyze and interpret data better than all others?
- Do you want to see with the eyes of an eagle?
- Do you want to think with the clarity of Sherlock?
- Do you know how to think deductively?
- Do you know how to utilize inductive reasoning?
- Do you want to add creative and innovative thinking to your cognitive toolbox?

You can! And — with a little bit of effort and plenty of practice — you *will!*

1

SHERLOCK'S BRAIN-ATTIC

*"I consider that a man's brain is originally
like a little empty attic, and you have to
stock it with such furniture as you choose...
It is of the highest importance, therefore,
not to have useless facts elbowing out the
useful ones."*
*–Arthur Conan Doyle in the Sherlock
Holmes mystery A Study in Scarlet*

Cleaning Out the Clutter

In order to think clearly like Sherlock, you need to have an open mind. You need a mind that is always ready for new input. What is it in today's world that accounts for clutter?

1. Multitasking — A Big "No-No"

    As much as you would like to believe that multitasking is the way to success in the 21st century, it's actually the very thing that's holding you back.

    Current research has shown that multitasking is a drain on your psychological and emotional well-being. According to Joseph Griffin of Northeastern University, "Multitasking is probably productivity's biggest enemy. It doesn't make us more efficient. It simply splits our time."

You might think you're doing two things at once; however, the reality is that your brain is forced to "load up" different contexts each time you switch between tasks.

Even our computer brethren are not immune to this – requiring them to constantly switch between tasks incurs a "context delay", slowing things down. The solution? Computers simply load up a big chunk of data required by the task instead of making multiple round-trips between the operating system and the program, and focus at the task at hand, making it much more efficient.

Between the time spent on tackling one task, and then taking on another new task, falls the shadow. The shadow represents the time lost. Clearly, that is not efficient.

Exercise: Multitasking is…

Try this on a sheet of paper or on your computer:

1. On line one, write "I know how to multitask."

2. On line two, write the numbers 1–20 in sequence.

The task above usually takes about twenty seconds.

1. Write the first letter of "**I** know how to multitask."

2. Move to the second line, and write #1.

3. Move back to the first line and write the "k" of "I **k**now how to multitask."

4. Move back to the second line and write #2.

> 5. Move back to the first line and write the "n" of "I
>   k<u>n</u>ow how to multitask."
>
> If you continue this futile task, you have now doubled the
> time these two tasks will take you.

There is an episode in the TV detective series, **Columbo,** in which
Columbo arrives at a crime scene carrying a hard-boiled egg, which
he is going to eat. He cracks the eggshell, breaks off pieces of it, and
munches on it as he examines the crime scene. After he is nearly
finished the egg, he is left with some of the hard-boiled egg and a pile
of eggshells in his hands. This segment was added for its comical
value, but is an example of multitasking. In the episode, he has
assistants there who relieve him of his breakfast leftovers.

2. Emotional Clutter — The static of hurt minds

Besides thought, also residing in your brain are two bean-
size objects called the amygdala. They regulate the
emotions. As you know, emotions are like little "beasties"
that awaken. Once that happens, they signal the various
parts of your body to respond according to the stimuli
presented cognitively. Sometimes that is helpful, such as
when you step out on the street and see a car careening
down the avenue right in your path. Sometimes, however, it
is not helpful when someone insults you, and the memory
of it hangs on, running rough shod through your cognitive
mind. That interferes with clear thinking. It may also cause
bias in your thinking and judgement.

Example of Emotional Control

You are at work concentrating on a task. Your co-worker walks by and says something that sounds insulting. There are several courses of action you can take:

1. You can stop what you're doing and question the co-worker.

2. You can continue with your work, and choose to ignore the comment, particularly if that co-worker does that all the time.

3. You can continue your task, although you will remember what the co-worker said, and plan on handling it later.

In the interest of maintaining focus on one and only one task at a time, options number 2 and number 3 are more ideal.

In the case of option 2, the emotional stimulus fails to have any bodily result. It is very difficult to do this, but it can be done.

In the case of option 3, you have trouble dismissing memory of the emotional import of the comment. Consequently, your emotions will be redirected to your body. You may get a slightly upset stomach, or the proverbial butterflies in your stomach. You have emotional "residue".

The most ideal technique for dealing with your emotional residue is to accept the fact that it is there, and let it float out of your current awareness — it may help if you envision a helium balloon. If your stomach feels uneasy, let it be so and move on. Emotions do pass. If they do not pass, your emotions may be sending you a message. For example, you may have to deal with that co-worker, but perhaps later on.

2

THE ULTIMATE POWER OF THE SENSES TO DEDUCT AND INDUCE

You might have heard this Sherlock Holmes story...

It began with the stairs leading up to the Holmes/Watson residence, 221B Baker Street. In this deduction, Holmes had remembered there were 13 steps on the way up. Watson wondered why he couldn't recall the number of steps. Yet Holmes seemed to know without even thinking about it.

Not terribly useful information, you say?

Suppose you were toting two large shopping bags in your arms, and you couldn't see the steps?

Senses are the only means by which people can interpret reality: sight, auditory, taste, olfactory, touch, and **time.** Most people rely almost exclusively on sight. In order to impress your friends, or maybe even a hero, it is vital to develop ALL your senses. That skill is invaluable to make deductions and develop inferences that are useful in formulating goals and modifying behavior.

Some examples from real life situations:

The Gas	The Finger Snap	Metal
Tanya was walking up the interior steps to an auditorium with about 100 people inside. She smelled gas. No one else around her on the stairway smelled it. So, Tanya located the janitor (who likewise could not smell it). He went into the basement and discovered that a pilot light was out. He then relit it.	*George was blind. He did not use a seeing-eye dog, so he had to rely on his other senses to compensate. One day when he was visiting a new friend. He and the friend went for a stroll in the backyard. The friend offered to take his arm and lead him around, but George just wanted to walk unassisted. There were some trees in the yard. In order to avoid walking into any of the trees, he put out his hand and snapped his fingers as he walked. George could hear the sound of his fingers snapping echo from a tree trunk.*	*Jamila was delayed at work so she called her husband and asked him to throw something into the oven for dinner. He liked to cook, so he made some meatballs and covered them with leftover canned tomato sauce from the refrigerator. He heated it up and served it over the meatballs upon Jamila's return. She took one bite, and removed their plates immediately. Her husband was confused. Jamila said there was metal in the tomato sauce. The metal from the can had blended with the acidic tomato sauce and – if eaten – could have been harmful to their bodies.*
No one knows what would have happened if her olfactory sense was not acute, but one can imagine.		

The Secret to Both Seeing and Observing

The above phenomena point out that, in order to observe things in our environment correctly, it is important to take all factors into consideration. This is why Sherlock Holmes always took all his senses into consideration when observing a situation.

The concept of actually *observing* everything you see is the focal point of clear thinking. Most of us only take in the skeleton image of what we see. We notice the man at the counter, but if we look away, and the man ducks down, and a different man continues the conversation, it's only human nature to *assume* that the man is the same, even though it's a completely different person.

(That's the joke behind the word "*assume*" – it makes an "ass" out of "u" and "me".)

Conversely, when Holmes looks at a staircase, he makes a mental note of how many stairs there are, in addition to other small details. If there is a railing, has something dropped on any of the steps? There are other things that most of us might view as irrelevant.

Arthur Conan Doyle, the creator of the Holmes character, was extremely brilliant in that he applied scientific wisdom to all of Holmes' actions.

This kind of acute awareness, when learned correctly, can be applied to solving problems of any kind, using strong, logical decision-making and imagination.

1. Exercise:

Take a close look at this picture. Note the objects in the room. What can you say about the personality of the room's occupant? What is missing from the picture? Is there anything wrong with it?

Personality: Slightly unkempt and rushed (failed to make the bed) Has trouble relaxing. (There is no crevice in the pillow from having sat there and read, for example. Also, there is no haddock for resting one's feet.)

Missing: The bow for the violin, and the bedroom slippers
If you are late for work and rush out, where are your slippers? Yes, you guessed it! They are on the floor.

<u>Problem:</u> No violinist would ever put a violin in a window. It would be exposed to the sun and its heat. Consequently, it would dry out and crack.

Sherlock might deduce that the owner doesn't play the violin, because he or she hasn't learned the basics of caring for the instrument. The owner is either lying or might be trying to show off. He or she might be a deceitful person, but is almost certainly egotistical.

2. Exercise:

Now it's your turn:

Note the design of this kitchen. Make some statements about the kitchen. First of all, it is clear that no one has moved into this house as yet. Judging only from the kitchen, what personality types might buy this house?

Statements about the kitchen:

_____

_____

_____

Personality Types:

_____

_____

*We assume that the sink is in the unseen portion of the room, as well as the dishwasher, and the oven.

Problems with the room for a prospective buyer:

_____

_____

_____

Noticing What's Not There…and What Detail Is Not Recalled

Have you ever heard the riddle about the ark? The question is this:

    A. "How many animals of each kind did Moses bring into the ark?"

If you answered "two" from listening to your past bedtime story, then your answer coincides with most people.

The fact is that the answer is zero, because Moses didn't round up any animals into the ark; that was Noah.

    B. "How many wheels does a car have?

If you answered "4", that's wrong. The steering wheel is also a wheel. So is the wheel of your spare tire in the trunk.

It takes a keen observational skill to notice all the words in a given sentence, and it also takes practice to allow all your senses to come into play when making an observation.

SELECTIVE LOOKING

Everyone has a way of "selective looking" — psychologists refer to this as "fast-thinking" and "slow-thinking". Fast-thinking uses your brain to make rapid, on the spot judgements, whether right or wrong, based on past experiences.

For example, everyone knows that artists use a shadowing effect to trick your brains into thinking that some objects are closer to you. In the real world, you know that objects appear smaller if they're further away, so when you look at an object in a picture, you make a quick inference telling you if they're up close or far away.

You can try this yourself by tinkering with PowerPoint images. Take an image of a railway or staircase and put in your picture. Now take a human image and place on top of the staircase. Take the same size image and place at the bottom to appear closer to you. Does the image on the top appear smaller? If so, your eyes are playing tricks on you.

Another popular optical illusion is the Marilyn Monroe/Albert Einstein picture. When you look at it from a distance away, the picture looks like Marilyn Monroe. However, as you look closer and become more aware of the features, it turns into Albert Einstein. Psychologists call this a hybrid image.

Neurobiologist, Mark Changizi, studied another phenomenon and pointed out that, when we look at look at an image, distance and lighting become factors in how the image is perceived. The background lighting in the famous "blue/black or gold/white dress" has to do with the background lighting and shadowing effects. When you're looking at a color that you perceive should be in a shadow, your brain automatically compensates by making the color look lighter.

Size and colors… it's all relative and your brain is always "autocorrecting" what you actually see. The information everyone takes in is all relative to outside information.

For example, look at two spots of the same size with no background. They appear to be the same size. However, if you place large circles around one, and small circles around the other, your brain will compensate by making the spots in the large circles seem smaller.

This is why dieticians tell you to put your meals on a small plate. That way, it will appear that you have more to eat.

> *"The difference between a flower*
> *and a weed is a judgement."*
> *-Wayne Dyer*

Perception is everything when it comes to what people see and hear. And it doesn't end with sight; your ears can also play tricks on you.

Similarly, when you combine what you see with your eyes and what you hear with your ears, your brain takes a shortcut and tells you that you might actually be hearing something different than that which is real. For example, if you listen to a recording of a man saying "bar, bar, bar" and you hear it again, it always sounds the same.

However, listen again to the same sound and watch a man on the screen making different moves with his mouth to form "b" or "f" sounds. What you will hear is distinctly different. Now, instead of hearing "bar, bar, bar", you're hearing "far, far, far". Psychologists call this the McGurk Effect.

Additionally, the "Tritone Paradox" discovered by Deutsch in 1986, points out that your brain focuses on only one tone at a time.

Deutsch produced two simultaneous tones, one a half an octave apart from the other. When the tone is played over and over, some people hear an ascending pattern, as if the musical notes are going up the scale. Others hear the opposite: an audible descending pattern. This phenomenon even works when musicians listen to it.

Why would that be? Psychologists say that the different perceptions come from how you perceive your own speaking voice, and the geographical location and languages in your environment when you were infants. Studies reveal a definite connection between the speech patterns you have been exposed to and how you perceive music.

3. Exercise:

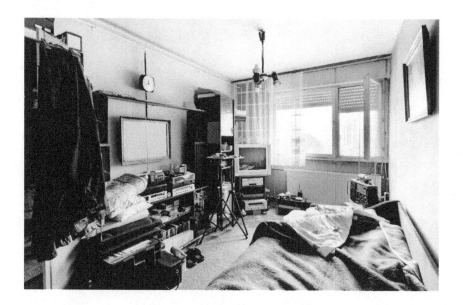

This is a fun exercise for you to do. After you take careful note of what's in the room, develop some deductions you can make about the personality of the occupant based upon the general appearance of the room. Also make some notes about what is missing in the room. Despite the clutter, there are important elements missing.

There are also some problems with the layout that can give you clues about the occupant. Make a prediction as to what will happen to the room in time. Time was included as a pseudo-sense, because it makes a difference in deduction. You will have a number of predictions.

Now, imagine the sounds and smells that emanate from that room. Notice that one of the windows is open. The occupant certainly needs it, along with a can of air freshener. There is, after all, insufficient ventilation. The sounds from the room, when the owner is there, will disturb the neighbors. (Note that you can see the window of another apartment through the bedroom window.)

3

SHERLOCK'S DEDUCTIVE & INDUCTIVE METHOD

THE SCIENTIFIC METHOD DEDUCTIVE REASONING

The Scientific Method is based upon **deductive reasoning**. If a hypothesis is proven to be true, it is "known information". If another situation arises, one can deduce that the same result will follow.

Deductive reasoning is all about looking at the entire situation, and then taking a few paces back to logically review by applying critical thinking. The "right choice" is the conclusion you will come up with based on the true facts found through critical thinking. The chapter about critical thinking will go into detail about how to do this.

Most people can't remember small details about any given situation. The fact that Holmes can logically come to a conclusion based on remembering detail seems like a trait that isn't even human. However, it really has to do with building a knowledge network by connecting new information with what you already know. There is also a chapter in this book devoted to increasing your memory by building your knowledge network.

A hypothesis is a premise that will or will not lead to a conclusion. For example, If P, then Y. If you plant a good seed on fertile ground, a plant will grow. Scientists use this technique to test out a theory. Drug companies use it to test experimental drugs. Once the relationship between the conclusion and the hypothesis is proven, the final results are known and can be predicted. Doctors use this method to diagnose illness. They perform tests on the patient, to see if they yield positive results. Once that happens, a treatment is prescribed. The scientific method is valid – usually.

Sherlock Holmes used deductive reasoning in his crime-solving:

> *"Once you eliminate the impossible,*
> *whatever remains, no matter how*
> *improbable, must be the truth."*
> *-Arthur Conan Doyle*

However, Sherlock used both deductive and inductive reasoning. His statement should be reworded:

> *"Within a set of known*
> *phenomena, once you have*
> *eliminated the impossible,*
> *whatever remains, no matter*
> *how improbable, must be*
> *true. If the entire set of known*
> *phenomena are eliminated as*
> *impossible, then the solution*
> *is simply unknown until new*
> *phenomena can serve as a*
> *solution is positively established."*

INDUCTIVE REASONING

Inductive reasoning occurs when a person analyzes the conclusion and realizes that it is <u>probable</u>, not absolute. No one possesses the entirety of reality. Everyone has experienced, or has learned a group of conclusions. The wise person is one who allows for the possibility that some of those conclusions may not be true. Before 1930, astronomers taught that there were eight planets circling the sun. Then they observed a slight "tug" on Neptune. It was caused by the slight gravitational pull from Pluto. Because it took so long for Pluto to revolve around the sun, it wasn't noticed before.

Inductive reasoning is the opposite of deductive reasoning. One observes the results, but allows for the possibility that conclusions may be false, <u>even if the hypothesis is true.</u>

A number of years back, a study was conducted which showed that men over forty who have creases in their ear lobes get heart attacks (hypothesis). The correlation derived from the testing reached statistical significance.

Men everywhere raced to their bathroom mirrors to analyze their ear lobes. Worry and anxiety ensued. Later on, more astute clinicians analyzed the testing procedure because the conclusion seemed illogical. A creased ear lobe does not cause heart attacks, nor it a symptom. Could a man's earlobe be straightened out, so the he wouldn't suffer a heart attack?

Follow-up analyses were conducted. Many examples did not fit the hypothesis, while others did. Many men with creased earlobes did get heart attacks. Other men with creased earlobes did *not* get heart attacks. When the clinicians examined the test procedures, they discovered that the study employed one of the weakest statistical tests used – the coefficient of correlation. Unfortunately, that statistic is very frequently used.

One cannot accept the result as absolute fact, unless he or she employs **deductive AND inductive reasoning.**

Sherlock used both deductive and inductive reasoning. In the **"Adventure of the Bruce Parkington Plans,"** a passenger heard a thud as the train sped along. The deduction Holmes made was that someone had fallen on the tracks. The next day, an inspection of the railroad tracks yielded no body. Sherlock reformulated the hypothesis, and came to the possible conclusion that a body fell on top of a train car. He used the inductive method to test out his theory, and it was proven.

The thud heard by the passenger means a body fell on the tracks <u>or it</u> <u>may <i>not</i> mean</u> that a body fell on the tracks.

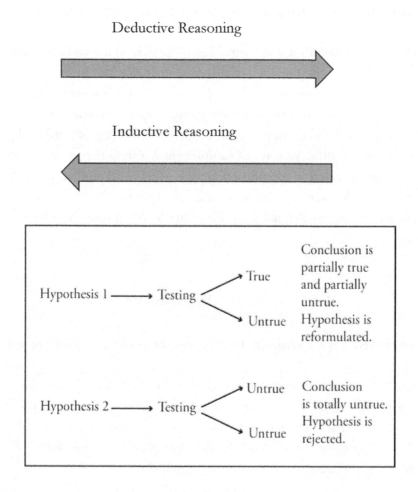

Deductive Reasoning

Inductive Reasoning

Hypothesis 1 ——→ Testing

→ True — Conclusion is partially true and partially untrue.

→ Untrue — Hypothesis is reformulated.

Hypothesis 2 ——→ Testing

→ Untrue — Conclusion is totally untrue.

→ Untrue — Hypothesis is rejected.

Business people, manufacturers, advertisers, and movie producers sometimes do not submit their premises to an inductive method in addition to the deductive method.

For example, a manufacturer presents a product to a group of test subjects and asks for their reactions. Most of the people laud the product, so the manufacturer feels confident and markets it. The product bombs. Sales plummet. What happened?

Clearly, the hypothesis needs reformulation or needs to be rejected. Most certainly the sampling and/or testing procedures were faulty.

The maker failed to use inductive reasoning which indicates that the conclusions reached by the test group may or may not be true. The test group may want to please the examiner, so it presents mostly positive reactions to the product presentation. That is called the "Hawthorne Effect". In this case, inductive reasoning prescribes that one must try different ways of sampling and testing the product. One might use a different sampling of people – people from various walks of life and different socioeconomic levels. This is called a stratified sample. He might also use a random sample, but it must be a large one.

INFERENCE AND OBSERVATION

An inference is a conclusion based upon the evidence. It is a process.

The "fast-thinking" part of your brain makes inferences. A certain amount of logical inference is necessary to make sense of what you see. Your brain collects the obvious facts and reacts to them based on your past experience. Your brains have evolved to use "fast-thinking", because it is necessary for survival.

If a man sees a tiger heading for him, he doesn't stop to count the stripes or calculate how fast the tiger might be advancing. His brain simply interprets danger, so he climbs up the nearest tree. He made a rapid inference derived from deductive reasoning that he would be safe.

Much to his surprise, the tiger climbs up after him! What happened? He took a chance, but used the incorrect inference, which is that he would be safe if he climbed the tree.

Scientists refer to "observation" as a way of accumulating informational facts by using all of your senses. When you look at something, in order to keep your brain from making the common "fast-thinking" shortcut, it's important to allow all your senses to come into play.

However, when you're trying to observe a situation in order to gather as many facts as possible, you need to be aware that the fast-thinking part of your brain might be getting in the way. Sometimes shortcuts can keep you from seeing the whole picture.

Using Sherlock Holmes' deductive *and* inductive method, the action may yield two results. One of those might be true, and the other false. The man in the example above inferred that climbing a tree would save him. Observation over time would teach the wise man that tigers can climb trees. Further study and observation of tigers' behaviors would instruct him that he would have to climb high — very high — to save himself. The fact of the matter is that tigers dislike climbing, and generally don't climb very high. They have trouble getting down.

In the story, **"A Scandal in Bohemia"**, Holmes explains to Watson the difference between observing and seeing. He points out that, even though Watson can see as well as Holmes, he never noticed how many stairs lead to their apartment.

1. **Exercises in Inference and Observation:**

   A. Read this passage:

      Imagine you are living in 15th century Romania. Your ruler is Vlad III Dracul (Dracula). You see many men impaled and placed on wooden stakes in the ground. Using deductive reasoning, you quickly infer that Dracula is cruel. Inductive reasoning, on the other hand, allows for true and untrue conclusions. So, you make allowances for the possibility that Dracula is not as cruel as you assumed.

Then you travel to Bulgaria. In Bulgaria, you observed that there are also many, many men impaled on stakes. Your premise needs reformulation. Why? It is because impalement was a very common form of civil punishment in that area during the 15th century. Your informed observations confirmed that.

B. Imagine you are an astute detective who uses developed observational and reasoning skills to solve two murders. Use deductive and inductive reasoning to figure them out.

The Bungalow Murder

A husband, his wife, and the husband's mother live in a bungalow-style home. As soon as the husband gets home from work, they eat a small leg of lamb for supper. The husband's mother is in her room. Sometimes she stays in her room during meals. After the couple has dined, the husband brings in a meal for his mother. The mother is found dead in her room, having been hit with a blunt object. During questioning, both the husband and the wife admitted that they intensely disliked the old woman. They both had a motive. However, they did not have the means to do it, because no murder weapon was found.

Using your most astute imaginary observational skills, where is the murder weapon and who did it?

The Old Mansion Mystery

There once was an early 19th century mansion located in the countryside. It was being used as a small retirement home for the elderly who did not need extra medical assistance. On the west end, there was an elevator used by both staff and residents. On the east end, there was a staircase, but it was broken down and usable. After the older folks dined, all the outside doors were locked. The residents went to their rooms on the elevator. Only Martha, from the kitchen staff, and one resident remained. Martha cleaned the dishes, and, Mrs. Gobel, the resident, was in the great room reading.

Suddenly, there was a thud and a moan emanating from the great room, so Martha ran out to see what happened. Mrs. Gobel lay dead on the floor with blood oozing from her head. Alongside, on the floor, lay a heavy stone bust of Socrates with bits of flesh and blood on it.

Now you, as the detective, are using your observational skills, as well as deductive and inductive reasoning. Deductively it seems clear that Martha did it. However, when you questioned some of the residents and the staff, it became apparent that Martha was very fond of Mrs. Gobel. Martha had the means to commit the crime, but no motive. Inductive reasoning allows for more than one possible conclusion. While the deductive reasoning seemed solid, inductively there was something wrong with the observations as presented. What was it? Once you know that, it will lead you to the possible culprit.

> Clue: Items leaning against the far wall in the broom closet near the great room are totally dislodged.

The Disappearance of Abbot Amadeus

There was once a small monastery situated on a mountain. On the grounds, there was a monastery building, a vegetable garden, and a small cemetery. Brother Anselm was the monastery cook. Now, Anselm sorely wanted to be the new abbot, but another monk, Brother Benedict, was slated to ascend to that role following Amadeus' death. One night, Brother Benedict died. Anselm was the next in line and he was excited about his prospective ascendancy. However, he didn't want to wait years and years for the death of Abbot Amadeus. That's when he decided to kill him. However, Anselm was also aware of the fact he couldn't poison the Abbot because he himself was the cook. He had to find another way. After much thought, he devised an ingenious plan. Late one night, Brother Anselm entered the Abbot's cell, and bludgeoned him to death. Then he cleaned up the cell, and disposed of the body.

The following day, the monks reported Abbot Amadeus missing. The monks searched everywhere. Then the police came and searched everywhere also. They even dug up the garden. No body was found. They then brought in cadaver dogs. The dogs didn't react to anything except the cemetery, and especially the recently dug grave of Brother Benedict.

Where was the body?

QUANTITATIVE AND QUALITATIVE OBSERVATION…

When making observations, scientists make sure they're noting both quantitative and qualitative observations. "Quantitative" refers to a specific number. Holmes' observation of the number of stairs that led to their apartment is an example of quantitative observation.

Once you're in the habit of being aware of your surroundings by using all your senses, you're better equipped to start making deductions.

FORMING THE HYPOTHESIS

The hypothesis, or educated "guess", needs to be drawn only after *all* pertinent information is obtained. That includes the "invisible" clues as well.

The idea, of course, is to first collect data in the proper way as described in the previous chapters. Now you're prepared to allow your brain to come up with a good hypothesis.

As Holmes says to Watson, "it's a foolish man who collects mindless data to clutter the mind attic".

Of course, there's more to that data than simply what you observe. It is necessary to pay attention to what's not there as well. An example of this is when Holmes was able to solve a crime case by noticing that the dog *did not* bark in the night.

OMISSION NEGLECT

As mentioned in the previous chapter, people tend to focus on only what's in front of them — only the information offered to them. Marketers love this!

Which cell phone would you prefer to buy?

Phone A: $100, Talk time 12 hours, Memory 16GB

Phone B: $150 Talk time 16 hours, memory 32GB

Most people would pick phone B.

What You May Not Have Noticed

What is the weight comparison? – Phone B is twice as heavy! And what if you found out later that the radiation was also twice as high with phone B?

People tend to only see and take note of the information given to them. It takes a little creativity to notice beneath the surface.

Being able to allow your brain to come to creative conclusions takes thinking outside the box, and allowing yourself to think creatively. Contrary to popular belief, creativity can be learned with practice. The use of creativity in developing your powers of deduction and induction is covered in Chapter 6.

Holmes teaches that the orderly "mind attic" is necessary. So when you're gathering information, it's important to "label" each of your memories in an orderly fashion.

Of course, with today's technology, most people don't bother to memorize details because they can always simply Google anything at any time.

THE GOOGLE EFFECT

There was actually a study done about the effect that Google has on peoples' memories. And, as you may have guessed, people do not tend to memorize facts like they used to before the Internet. However, the interesting phenomenon is that people, instead, were likely to memorize *where* they found the information. This, in the long run, can actually be even more useful, because they can extend that which is in their minds to that which is in the cloud.

As you recall your memories in your mind, you will probably notice a lot of incidences where the fragrance or odor of a particular memory persists. This is because the sense of smell, being tied the most with human emotion, is the strongest link to memory.

Now that you have all your facts – the pieces of the puzzle are drawn together from proper observation. Now it's time to begin deducing in order to make the right decision.

The hypothesis isn't simply drawn out of thin air. It is an "educated guess" that comes from a mind clear of clutter.

This is why Holmes will take a step back before developing his hypothesis.

How to Take a Step Back

Have you ever noticed that when you're distracted with several things and *not* living in the present moment, you're not as happy as you might be just enjoying where you are?

This is a lesson that Holmes has taught. If you remember how it was when you were a child, when you were watching an ant climb on your hand and wondering what it would be like to be that ant, or picking the petals of a flower and examining every detail. If you remember how happy you were when the thoughts in your head showed how life seems very simple?

As adults, most people are usually so caught up in their responsibilities and plans about what they need to do next, that they fail to live in the present. It doesn't have to be that way. In fact, studies show that people actually can get more accomplished when they put all their focus on one thing at a time.

Conversely, as children, your mind is curious, always asking questions. This sense of constant curiosity is what you need to get back. It's the very essence of what keeps you sincerely motivated and happy.

And, as a child, you believed you can be anything you want to be. If you ask a five-year-old if she thinks she's creative, the answer would be an emphatic "yes". How many adults do you suppose would have the same answer?

Believing that you can get what you want is an extremely powerful tool! Children are believers. They believe that they can accomplish whatever they set out to do. You need to take a page from their book. In fact, the power of belief was proven in a recent study. People were asked to wear white coats, and comparisons were drawn on their cognitive ability to solve problems. Surprisingly, the people who wore white coats actually came up with conclusions easier and faster than those who didn't. The white coat simply made them feel smarter like doctors. Those results were astounding!

Allowing Your Brain to Breathe

Additionally, it's necessary to give your brain a "breather" and focus on something that's less cognitively taxing. When this is done, the part of the brain that deactivates actually causes more creative juices to work the creative part of the brain, and the answer appears.

As mentioned in a previous chapter, a good way to clear your mind of clutter is to walk through nature. This is an excellent "mind breather". The relaxation techniques that Holmes would engage in were usually playing the violin, going to a museum, or simply sitting down and smoking his pipe.

In fact, the first step that Holmes would take was to sit and smoke. "This is the 3-pipe problem", he'd say to Watson. And, at the end of smoking the third pipe, the answer would come to him.

Some people decide to "sleep on it", which has also proven to be effective, because it allows your brain to come up with the right answer.

Reaching the right hypothesis is the most critical part of deducing and inducing conclusions.

FRAMEWORK TIPS OF FORMING
AN EFFECTIVE HYPOTHESIS

- Begin with your conclusion.

  Most people try to frantically work towards a conclusion. However, Holmes teaches that the secret lies in the ability to reason backwards. The normal way of thinking is from cause to effect. However, when people focus first on the outcome and reason backwards, the result is inductive thinking, as opposed to synthetic thinking. Detectives will look for clues, which lead to root causes.

  Reasoning backwards is more effective because you wind up with one hypothesis, rather than several, to test.

  The primary scientific method is:
  - State the problem – write it down or say it out loud. Holmes would state his problem to his associate, Watson, which served to clarify the problem in his mind.
  - Collect your research data.
  - Clear your mind and give form to your hypothesis.
  - Conduct tests to prove or disprove your hypothesis.

- Clear your mind before approaching a problem.

  If you have a theory in your mind before observing the facts, your emotions can tend to skew the possible result. A clear mind is necessary in order to approach your problem objectively.

- Collect satisfactory data.

  Make sure you have all the data necessary before drawing conclusions. Also, steer clear of allowing your emotions to sway how you interpret your data. Collect only facts.

- Eliminate nonessential data and focus on vital information.

  This takes practice. Making sure your mind is clear before tackling a problem is the first step in being able to notice what is important and weed out the trivial noise.

- As Holmes says, "Once you eliminate the impossible, whatever remains, no matter how improbable, must be the truth."

  In your observation process, notice consistent patterns between outstanding and inferior achievement. Any fact that remains is critical. And often, it's something that you never would have expected. Here again, it's important to observe with a blank mind, which enables you to draw a more accurate conclusion.

  Observe what's contrasting when an obstacle occurs, and when it doesn't. Then, try to notice consistent differences. If you notice something that is consistently different, then this is a critical clue.

  Reflect upon your emotional reaction to a person, a place, or an object. Ask yourself why you react that way. Your emotions can provide you with invaluable information.

Once the clues are confirmed, it's time to establish the root cause of the problem.

4

INCREASING YOUR POWERS OF OBSERVATION

The following exercise is a modification of a mindfulness meditation particularly geared toward increasing your observational awareness through the use of your senses.

You can spend as little as five minutes a day to practice meditation, and it's a great stress-reliever in the middle of a busy day.

How do you do it?

Just Follow These Six Easy Steps

1) Sit in a position where you are comfortable, but not so comfortable that it's easy to go to sleep. While the traditional martial arts position is the "seiza", sitting on your legs with your knees in front, most people are likely to find this uncomfortable. Don't sweat it. You can also just sit with your legs crossed as you did as children. Or, if you have back trouble or any ailment that might get in the way of feeling comfortable sitting upright, then feel free to sit in a

comfortable chair resting slightly back, but upright enough to stay awake. Now focus on one point, straight ahead.

2) Start taking deep breaths. Be aware of your breathing. Breathe deeply, in through your nose, out through your mouth. Be aware of how your belly expands with every inhalation. Be aware of how your anxiety is leaving your body with every exhalation. Try to make the first couple of breaths take the longest, perhaps counting to five before you exhale. Then start breathing normally, but stay aware of how relaxed and stress-free your body feels with every exhalation.

3) Aim your thoughts towards your body, and focus on how relaxed your toes feel, how relaxed your legs and thighs feel, working your way up your body. Try to envision your anxiety actually leaving your body in a cloud of dust. If you start to think about the stresses of the day, don't worry. It happens to everyone. Just try your best to refocus your attention to your breathing and your body.

4) Close your eyes and focus on all the sounds outside yourself. The cars on the road, a bird tweeting, the wind, the sound of a radio in the background, etc. Return to the sounds of your gentle breathing.

5) Open your eyes. Add the visual elements you see in your room and out of the window to your mental list.

6) Now, without looking out, write down all the things that your senses have "told" you.

Practical Applications

Learning to observe and notice things that others do not see will take a lot of practice. You might use the following notations to help you grasp the idea of how to use your senses more effectively to become more mindful and aware.

- Take note of your surroundings.

Most people tend to only see what they came to see. When you walk into your office and you don't usually notice that someone left a full cup of coffee on the desk you pass. That kind of information could have been handy before you inadvertently back into it, causing it to dump all over you.

- Take note of your feelings – how does your observation affect you?

You notice that the person next you in the theatre is wearing strong perfume and you remember your allergies. Now you can make the decision to sit somewhere else before your ability to watch the movie is impeded with a barrage of sneeze attacks.

- Be aware of how your "unintentional blindness" can block the truth in how you might perceive a particular situation.

Remember there's no such thing as multitasking. Don't allow that bad habit to block other things from your conscious perception. As you make a decision to focus more on the "peripheral" things that others don't see, the result of how it makes a difference in the way you make decisions may completely surprise you.

Learning how to observe and be aware of your surroundings will help you to become mindful with the use of all your senses. Pay attention to how your senses affect the choices you make, and you will begin to foster a greater awareness of your environment.

If you can sharpen your senses and powers of observation, you can impress everyone in your office with your newfound "Sherlock" skills. Here is an example from real life:

> *At work, Emma's desk was piled up with papers, along with the computer, pens, and an appointment book. Usually, everyone kept their office doors open during work. One day, Emma noticed that her Sharpie pen was missing. She also noticed that a fellow employee, Patrick, had left his notepad on her desk. When she went into Patrick's office to return his notepad, Emma's Sharpie pen was on his desk. On the next day, Emma noticed a cell phone on her desk that wasn't hers. She also noticed that her stapler was missing. Using some inductive reasoning, she brought the cell phone to Patrick and asked for the return of her stapler. Patrick was a sub-conscious pack rat! When others complained about missing items, Emma told them: "Exchange one of Patrick's things left in your office for your missing items." Everyone was amazed.*

Get in the habit of observing everything around you, not just seeing.

Did you ever take a walk from your hotel and have trouble finding your way back? If so, then you're one of millions who is in the habit of seeing and not observing. Take mental notes of your surroundings – what color is the building and what landmarks are nearby? Once you're in the habit of observing, and not just seeing, it's easier to make deductions.

5

TAKING NOTES TO
IMPROVE ATTENTIVENESS

Most people don't pay complete attention to anything around them. As mentioned earlier, this is largely because of multitasking in today's society. However, taking notes is one positive habit to acquire that will point you in the right direction.

Take Field Notes during the Day

Note-taking is a good habit acquired by many successful business people. Remember in school how you would remember things better when you wrote them down? If you were to simply listen to a lecture and not take notes, the average person retains only about 10% over the long-term. (This is based on a study of students retaining seminar information – they reported 90% forgotten points after 14 days.)

"We remember what we understand; we understand only what we pay attention to; we pay attention to what we want."
- Edward Bolles

The quote above makes mention of your different kinds of memory. Taking field notes will help to ensure understanding, but you can't possibly take notes unless you're paying close attention.

HOW MEMORY WORKS

As you may already know, everybody has both a short-term and a long-term memory.

Short-Term Memory

Did you ever try to memorize a phone number? You know how challenging this is to hold in your memory for any length of time. The average person can hold only seven pieces of information at a given time; hence, we have 7-digit phone numbers. Put a foreign area code before the number, and see how much more difficult it is. Information that needs to be *learned* has to be transferred to long-term memory.

Human beings have the amazing ability to throw out useless information later on, and it is not committed to long-term memory. Computers don't do that. Even when some information is deleted, the computer holds on to it for a while until it "gets around to" deleting it. That is why investigators can often retrieve deleted information.

Long-Term Memory

This is whatever information you have learned and can remember. The transformation process from short to long term memory happens one of two ways:

- Through repetition, "rote learning"
- Through understanding, (connecting a relationship with the new information to what you already know)
- Through the strength of the emotions experienced in conjunction with the information

Both ways of learning are effective; however, studies conducted on learning and memory always reveal that going back and reviewing the information learned makes a substantial difference. And this, of course, is the reason for taking notes. Experts tell you that the best time to review your notes is **within a day or two** after the event.

A study conducted on forgetting textbook material with students revealed about 17% retention after 63 days. The problem with remembering course material is that most people tend to only remember that which is of interest to them. Studies show that when people can link what they discover to long term goals, it's more apt to stay in their conscious minds.

For example, if you're remembering notes from school, try to note the fact that what you're learning can be implemented in your future career. If you're writing a book, then try to takes notes with an idea of what you would write about.

Keys to Remembering

- Pay attention by choice. Most people tend to listen only to the things they're interested in. As for you, make a deliberate choice to remember.
- Use visualization: Take a mental "snapshot" of what you're trying to remember. For example, let's say that you are trying to cut up some cardboard boxes with an X-Acto knife. So, you start cutting them and put the pieces aside. Then you take the next box, and reach beside you on the floor. The X-Acto knife is missing! Where is it? Work stops as you search all over for it. Now, if you take a mental "snapshot" of the knife and where you put it every time you lay it down, you will remember where it is when you need it again.
- Tie the new information to what you already know. This puts the idea in a "file" in your brain. Sherlock Holmes referred to the brain as the "attic" of knowledge. Make sure your "brain attic" is neat and orderly.
- Repetition and review: This is where note-taking comes in. Make sure you review your notes and picture again in your

mind what you've learned. Rephrase it in your own words so that it makes perfect sense to you.

If you're the kind of person whose mind tends to wander, then this is for you. Taking notes while you're on-site or in the field is a way of keeping your attention on the here and now. Scientists recommend taking field notes throughout the day wherever you are.

A study done by Carrell in 2002 analyzed the effects of note-taking with students in various subjects. Results revealed that 67% of the students improved on the listening test, and 75% agreed that they could retain more information from the lecture when taking notes.

There are three main types of field notes, all of which you'll want to utilize.

TYPES OF FIELD NOTES

- Jotted Notes

    These are the most resourceful, and you'll want to make sure you always a have a small, pocket-size pad of paper with you. Jotted notes can be taken in the following format:

    When on-site, jot down a brief description of what you want to make mention of. Also, be sure to note how you feel at that time. Remembering your emotional state will help you link the incident to a memory.

    Later, review your notes, and draw distinctions between what you observed, how you felt, and your analysis of the situation.

- Mind Notes

On occasion, you will not be in a position to take jotted notes, so this is where you want to take mind notes as accurately as possible. Take a mental image of how you feel, including all your senses Remember smells, recall feelings, remember what sounds you might hear, and link that information to what you can see, or even taste if it applies. Take note of your initial reactions, how you might feel if roles were different.

Now, take your thoughts and feelings a step further and ask yourself why.

"Why did I react that way?" or "why was he trying to avoid answering my question?" This will help when it comes time to draw connections and come up with the right answer.

Once you start noticing and paying attention to the world around you, you can start turning your observations into ideas. Remembering *how you feel* and *taking in all sense-derived information* are most important here.

- Interview Notes

Taking notes while talking with someone will naturally require permission first from the person you're investigating. Don't be creepy. Be sure to give your full attention to the person you're talking to, and don't interrupt. It's good to stay on friendly terms, as long as you're not getting too personal.

Organizing Your Field Notes

Notes can be taken in the form of text, pictures or charts, whichever makes the most sense at the time. You'll want to make sure you include the following for each incident you're noting:

Things to include in your notes…

- Time and place
- Sensory perceptions, using all your senses
- Specific facts noted – what happened as you see it
- Your personal response – how did you feel at the time? How did others feel? Did you learn anything from this observation?
- Take note of language used and summarize the event
- Ask yourself questions about what else you want to find out

Try to focus on what's relevant to the situation. When you acquire the habit of taking notes wherever you are, you're training your brain to pay attention.

So what can you do first?

Start by trying to pay close attention to small details. For example, in a park, examine the behavior of a duck. Take note of when they fly and in what direction. Try to draw a parallel to why.

You can also pay close attention to people at work, taking note of little habits of each individual.

Once you're in the habit of putting details down on paper, it will become second nature, and your brain will automatically start thinking.

6

CREATIVITY AND IMAGINATION
IN PROBLEM-SOLVING

In order to think like Sherlock Holmes, you may need to look at the situation in a new and unusual way. Many people use a process known as lateral thinking.

LATERAL THINKING

Lateral thinking is the use of a creative and indirect approach to solve a problem. Today, it is often called "Thinking Outside the Box". One must do that when all obvious deductions fail. Induction, as seen earlier, often calls for reformulation of the hypothesis. This can entail a great deal of creativity.

<u>Exercise A:</u>
Let's say a man is found stabbed to death in his living room. One knows that through deduction, because there is a large gaping wound in his back. No murder weapon is present that matches the size of the wound. Earlier, the inhabitants opened the front door and noted that there had been a fierce winter storm, with lots of snow and ice. So, no one had left the house that day. What was used as the murder weapon?
(Answer after this chapter)

Comedians and cartoonists use lateral thinking very frequently:

In the image above, note that there can be two different interpretations of the term "red tape". Below is another example.

No answers will be provided for the next two exercises.

Exercise B: A car thief steals a BMW and races it up a street. The police stop all traffic at the end of the street and check all the vehicles. The only vehicles in the line-up are: open bed pickup truck, an SUV, a Ford, a Toyota, a tractor-trailer, a motorcycle, and a Mazda. There are no side streets on that particular block. Where is the BMW?

Exercise C: A man, who has a pilot's license, threatens to kill his wife. A few weeks later, he takes her on a flight over a forested area. The plane crashes. The wife dies, but the pilot walks away with just a few bruises. When the police checked, all the parachutes aboard were unopened. They had not been used. They thought perhaps the man had his own parachute, so they searched the man, and checked the forest around the plane, including the treetops, and found none. Could the man have killed the wife? If so, how?

Why Is It That Children Seem to Have Better Creative Abilities?

There are several reasons why children will allow their creative abilities to branch out, whereas adults hold back.

- They're not yet embarrassed to do silly things.

As adults, you have learned for years to follow the rules. "Color within the lines", they said. Sit up straight, take breaks when the bell rings, pay your bills on time, keep your car insured... etc. If not, heaven forbid, there will be consequences to pay.

Experts define maturity as "acting appropriately" and "conforming to

47

social rules".

As adults, you have also learned that it's just not appropriate to slurp spaghetti or finger-paint on the walls. As adults, you can see hours of scrubbing down the walls later – but you miss the creativity of the moment.

Read this true-life example below and note how a child develops creative ideas:

A husband tells his wife he is going to bring the boss home for dinner. She tells her little girl to play. The woman placed a few Cornish hens on the counter, and then prepared some potatoes and beans, and put them into the oven. Next, she reached for the Cornish hens. The Cornish hens were missing! She and her husband frantically searched the kitchen and even the dining room. No Cornish hens! So, the poor woman started to make some quiche. Then they helped pick up the little girl's toys. The "toys" consisted of a large open box turned on its side. Inside, she had a few little dolls, and…. the Cornish hens! The little girl explained that she was serving supper to her little dollies in their "kitchen". (the cardboard box)

Yet, let's face it —— being a mature adult all the time is downright boring. The problem is that we have allowed reality to beat down our natural urge to be creative.

In reality, however, adults have the brain power to actually be more creative than children – and that's been clearly demonstrated by movie producers and cartoonists.

The underlying reason that children are more creative is that they haven't learned yet how to be embarrassed about their behavior.

TECHNIQUES FOR DEVELOPING CREATIVITY THROUGH LATERAL THINKING

When you're with your friend at dinner, why not start acting like a different person and start talking with a strange accent?

Example A

When the store clerk asks: "How are you today?", respond with something like: "Oh…I'm feeling about 60%. And you?"

Example B

When you are walking down the street, stop and look up. Note how many other people will do the same.

Example C

Join forces with a friend. In the back of a full elevator in an apartment building, start up a conversation with your friend in a loud whisper. The imaginary scenario is the theft of some expensive jewelry. Start by whispering: "Where did you hide the jewelry?"
Friend: "Oh, I buried it just under the topsoil in that patch of woods in the back of this building."
You: "We will have to go back later and move it somewhere safer, after the cops leave."

When you get to your apartment, look out of your back window to see how many people are searching the woods!

Example D

Let's say that you and three of your friends go to a restaurant. The wait time for a table is an hour. While you wait, you notice that there are a few small tables in the bar room. So, you ask if you can wait for the table in the bar. The hostess says that is all right. Then you and your friends grab a small table in the bar. You notice that another small table in the room is empty. You and one of your friends picks up the little table and lines it up with the table you commandeered. There, you have it! A table for four in the bar room. Lo and behold, a waitress shows up and takes your order! Time spent: fifteen minutes.

Example E

Now, let's say that you and your date go to a fancy restaurant. "No, we don't have any reservations," you say. You are then told the wait is at least two hours long. Try a little "fun" lie. Say to your host: "Don't you know who my date it? She's Phyllis Affleck, the sister of Ben Affleck (the famous actor)." Suddenly, you and your date are seated right away. Of course, Ben Affleck doesn't have a sister. Even if the host thought he knew that, he has now been thrown into doubt and gives you two a table.

- Children are trusting.

As much as it's a good thing to become self-reliant to some extent, growing to depend on no one but YOURSELF also breeds skepticism of others.

As adults, we need to remember that trusting each other and forming human bonds will allow us to be aligned with how we really are and who we were meant to be.

- A child's life is simple.

Sometimes, a simpler life with no responsibilities allows you to be more creative and see the world as it is. As a child, you might see something new and want to explore it. As responsible adults, you see a swimming pool and think about how cold you'll be when you get out, especially if it's a windy day with no sun. If you think about hiking around a lake, and you remember that the way back might be less enjoyable if you get tired.

Conversely, the child on the swing simply wants to pump as high as he or she can, taking in every moment of the feeling of being free with the wind against his or her face.

How to Embrace Your Inner Child

- Decide to do something outrageous.

Forget about thinking how embarrassing something might be. There have been some instances where people have done something creative that you might feel was embarrassing.

For example, one day a man stood blindfolded on a busy street with a sign hung on his body: "Please hug me." "How outrageous," you might think. "I could never do that!" Yet this proved to be an extremely important psychological phenomenon.

For a long time, the man just stood there with arms outstretched while people walked by and ignored him. Some, of course, pointed and giggled, and others just stared and walked on.

Then, finally, one woman came up and gave him a hug. Once she got the ball rolling, more people came up, and it wasn't before long there was a line of people waiting to hug the stranger.

Imagine being the first one to think of something like that, and being brave enough to carry it out. Embracing your inner child takes bravery as an adult because you need to get past the worry of what others might think.

- If you have a child, try making up an imaginative bedtime story.

This will not only spark your own imagination, but your child will enjoy it tenfold.

He or she will love it and look forward to a new story all the time.

> *"To stimulate creativity, one*
> *must develop the childlike*
> *inclination for play."*
> —*Albert Einstein*

Engage in an artistic craft.

> *"Every child is an artist.*
> *The problem is how to*
> *remain an artist once we grow up."*
> —*Pablo Picasso*

What seems natural to a child becomes self-doubt in an adult.

Studies on children's creativity reveals that an adult's attempts at self-control often gets in the way of imagination. The studies refer to the "executive function" of your brain that tends to want to always follow the rules and may hold you back from saying inappropriate things.

The studies showed that "practice in pretending" allows creativity to flow naturally. Children love to pretend to be Batman or Wonder Woman. And, the more they get outside of themselves, the greater their imagination.

You can allow your imagination to take off by developing artistic skills. It might help to join a class where you can get feedback from others. This will help you build your confidence as a creative being.

Drawing or painting a picture while listening to music can really spark creativity and thinking. Make nonsense lines based on what you hear and then draw something from them.

Or, as an alternative, simply redecorate your home. Change around the furniture, or paint the walls. Adding color to your environment can literally add color to your life.

- Learn something new. You can even simply make the decision to learn a new word every day. The more you learn, the more you'll want to learn.

Some people like to learn a new language and then visit another culture. Learning more about other cultures – whether in person or in books – is a great way to inspire creativity.

- Read!

Reading or taking in new information of any kind is a tremendous imagination enhancer. With the technology of today, you don't even have to take time out to read a book. You can order audio books and listen on your way to work, or watch informative YouTube videos while you're working out at home.

THE BENEFITS OF NATURE

Another thing that can give you a huge creativity boost is the simplicity of nature.

Studies have found that a simple 20–minute walk through nature can help inspire creativity and solve problems. People who have been stumped on solving problems have reported that the answer will just "appear" after a walk through nature.

Additionally, it has been reported that even changing your screen saver on your computer to a nature scene can give you a cognitive boost.

A new study on this issue was conducted by Ruth Ann Atchley, Associate Professor of Cognitive & Clinical Psychology at the University of Kansas. The creativity test was called the "Remote Associates Test", and given to 60 backpackers, divided into four groups.

Another group of 60 backpackers received the same test, but taken at a different time – four days into the hike. The second group who were deeply immersed in nature scored 50% higher in creativity. Ages of subjects ranged from 18 to over 60, so it appears that age doesn't make a difference, because the results were always higher when subjects were surrounded by nature.

> *"Nature is a place where our*
> *mind can rest, relax and let*
> *down those threat responses."*
> *–Ruth Ann Atchley*

The conclusion is that, when you're forced to immerse yourself only in the common stress that modern life offers, your creative juices and positive thoughts are sapped.

- A walk through a local park can spark creativity and give you a definite cognitive boost. The outdoors are also better for your health.

Of course, more time is even better if you can manage it. The decision to ride a bicycle to get to your destination rather than using public transportation is a good one if you can get on a route that exposes you to natural scenes. These days, many places have nature trails that extend for miles.

Walking and being in the great outdoors does a body much more good than just sparking creativity and cognitive abilities. A recent study on health discovered that depression was reduced by 71% in those who regularly take a nature walk.

- A nature walk helps your analytical ability.

According to the *Journal of Environmental Psychology*, a 20–minute walk is all you need to restore your body from stress. New ideas appear and your ability to analyze problems is improved after a walk through nature.

How can you start being more creative? Just start trusting in yourself. You are a unique gift from the Universe with unique ideas. Don't let your self-doubt get in the way. Look at the world through the eyes of a child, and think about the design flaws. What's needed out there? Then imagine a wonderful solution.

You can stimulate others to think, and they will be impressed with your abilities. For example, if you are in charge of a team meeting and the members await your arrival with sleepy-eyed and bored expressions. How are you going to stimulate thought and solution-based results? It will make you look smarter than others, and may even lead to a promotion.

Arrive with a bunch of helium balloons! Laughter will ensue and bored expressions will disappear. Point to someone and ask for a contribution. That person has been singled out, so he or she will present something. Then hand that team member a balloon. Everyone will laugh, but they will get the idea. One by one, they will make contributions, and one by one, each will get a balloon. At the end of the meeting your team will be so stimulated that they will develop new ideas and solutions. All of you will be "thinking outside the box". They will release that inner child hiding within each one of them. What's more, everyone will be impressed with you, much like Watson was with Sherlock Holmes.

Answer to Exercise A: An icicle hanging from the front door portal.

7

IMPROVING YOUR MEMORY SKILLS

While putting notes down on paper and reviewing them regularly is a good start for boosting your memory, there's actually a "shortcut" method that should be noted here. It's the fun alternative to "rote learning". And, it's also much more effective.

The mind palace concept, also known as the "memory palace technique" has its origin in ancient Greece. Years ago, people relied on this technique to remember. And a good memory, by the way, was much more mandatory centuries ago.

Today, people are spoiled with calculators, cellphones and the internet. Why try to memorize a grocery list when your spouse can text it to you? Why try to memorize Mom's phone number when you have direct dial on your phone? After a while, you might forget the actual number. Isn't that embarrassing?

But wait a minute... does this mean that the people from the 1800's had better memories than we do now? Do we really want to allow our brains to memorize *less* as the years go by?

Not a good idea... just think of where that might lead.

According to Greek mythology, the Greek poet Simonides of Ceos came up with mind palace system after a tragic situation at a banquet he had attended. He was supposed to meet two men. However, when he arrived, the two men had been victims of the hall collapsing.

Everyone at the banquet had been crushed, and Simonides was asked to remember the names of the bodies.

This led to an important discovery. Simonides thought of each of the victims based on where they were sitting at the banquet, remembering the names of each one as associated with their place at the table. This was the birth of the "loci method", later called "the memory palace".

Wow! Who would have thought? The fact is that the human mind, while having difficulty memorizing a list of items, can actually remember space very accurately.

Think about it. Do you remember the address of your childhood house? Maybe not. However, think about the special orientation in the house. Remember? Most likely, you remember the rooms, the furniture and which way to turn from the front door to find your own bedroom.

Imagine how Simonides must have felt as he witnessed the crushed bodies of the banquet hall. He had an emotional response with each body as he remembered the name of the person who was supposed to be in that position.

Ah, so maybe the idea is to combine emotion with spatial orientation! This very popular technique grew to be even more popular among monks all through the Middle Ages, when people had to rely on memory to commit religious texts to memory.

In today's society, we all have some "place" that's familiar to us. Most likely, you will actually remember the spatial orientation of every house you've ever lived in. And, did anything that was really emotional event happen in some of those rooms you remember? Bingo! Combine emotion with space, and you have an image you just can't get out of your mind.

Exercise A: Solve a Mystery

A billionaire had a dinner party at his mansion. He invited all his children and grandchildren, and a few new guests, including Sherlock Holmes. The guests sat near the end of the table. He threw these dinners often, so everyone sat in the same chairs each time. After everyone was seated, the maidservant came out with a few bottles of wine. She poured the wine into everybody's glass for the traditional toast. The billionaire presented his toast, and everyone took a sip. Suddenly, Woodruff Woodcliff leaped up, and grabbed his throat. He gurgled, foamed at the mouth, and fell over dead. Everyone rushed over to him and chaos ensued. Woodruff had been poisoned! Even though everyone else had the same wine, only Woodruff died. Sherlock used the mind palace technique, and remembered where people were sitting. He then ran over to Woodruff's wine glass and sniffed. It smelled like bitter almonds. "Cyanide," he said. How was it possible that only one drink had cyanide? Who killed Woodruff?

Sample Application of the Mind Palace Technique

Suppose your spouse gives you a list of things to get at the grocery. In normal circumstances, you'd have to write down each item. But she's telling you on the phone, and you're in your car driving with no way to write anything down.

How can you remember?

The technique here is to link the item with the space you remember.

Picture your house, for example:

The first item: Three gallons of milk.

You imagine this milk in the driveway of your house – milk going bad in the sun.

The next item: Six bars of soap.

Now you're visualizing the soap bars on your doorstep. They are starting to suds over and you're worried that people might slip and fall if they approach house.

The next item: Twelve ears of corn.

In your imagination, you position the corn in the next area of your house, the entryway. Corn is growing all over the entrance to your house as soon as you open the door. Now, anyone who's lucky enough to get past all that soap, has to deal with rows of corn.

The next item: Two bags of cookie dough.

You get past the corn and enter the living room where you have placed the cookies. There they are, sitting on top of the TV. But, oh, the cookies are cooking themselves and they smell delicious! Only, they're melting all over the TV and you want to find a way to salvage the delicious cookies and your TV as well.

The next item: Twelve bunches of bananas.

This is, in itself, a boring item. But you have planted this item in the kitchen in your home. You visualize a bowl of bananas on the kitchen table. And, there are more bananas in the kitchen sink. You look in the dishwasher – more bananas! They're all over your kitchen, peeling the skins off each other and dancing naked.

And the last item: Four boxes of cereal.

At this point you've waded through the bananas and have made your way to the garage, where you're visualizing cereal boxes in the garage.

Each box is crying out, "Pick me, pick me!" and you laugh as you think about which one of the boxes has the most outrageous cry for help.

Sherlock Holmes used this technique in the play, **"The Holmes of BCC/Masterpiece Sherlock"** played by Benedict Cumberbatch. Of course, he masters the technique in an instant, because he's been practicing this method for years. You can master it, too. It might take a little persistence in the beginning, but the more you work at it, the more efficient your mind palace will help you to remember everything you command it to recall.

At first glance, you might think that this technique can only be effective with a small grocery list. However, people have been known to use this system for remembering even a full deck of cards. World Memory Champion, Dominic O'Brien, used the technique to memorize 24 decks of cards in sequence. Additionally, the memory palace technique has been used to learn a foreign language or memorize a presentation.

So How Can You Start Utilizing This Technique in 5 Easy Steps?

1) Choose the place you want to commit to memory — your "palace".

   Remember, the more familiar your palace, the better the technique will work. Choose a familiar location in which you can instantly visualize every room.

   Also, always choose the same route to walk through your palace. If your normal walkthrough is from the kitchen to the garage, then always go that way – don't alternate and enter through the garage.

Your home is only the most obvious place to choose. You can also use the technique with your school, your work place, or a local park with which you're familiar.

2) What features in your palace are memorable or distinctive?

Commit to memory the items in your palace that are always there; the front door, the TV, the couch, the entry way, etc. Practice your walkthrough by going on a memory walk in your mind. However you visualize, it should always be the same: from left to right, front to back, however you prefer it. Certain distinct features in each room should capture your attention; the TV in the living room, the large mirror over the piano… you get the idea. As you continue your "mental walkthrough", take mental pictures as you go. You'll be surprised how easily you can remember these "memory slots" to recall events or items later when you use the technique.

3) Make sure the route in your memory palace is firmly imprinted.

You will probably want to conduct a walkthrough several times in your mind before attempting to plant items to remember. You'll want to know your palace like the back of your hand. This is the most important thing: your memory palace *must* be **100% imprinted** on your mind.

If you're beginning this technique for the first time, try starting with only ten locations in your palace, and conduct the walkthrough in the same way over and over. Notice the stationary items that are always there. It can help if you say out loud the names of each room and the items you see.

Another thing that might help a newbie practice this method is to first write down the sequence of all the rooms, preferably in a graphic. We all actually think in pictures, so this will serve as a shortcut.

As you conduct the mind walkthrough, make sure you're always looking at the items in each room from the same point of view.

This step is the most important to build the foundation of your memory palace. You might believe you're done, but do it again anyway. You must be 100% confident of where each room and key objects are in the room in order for the technique to work.

4) Now it's time to put your palace to work.

All of the rooms with associated objects you've just committed to memory are called "memory pegs". As described in the example earlier in this chapter, make everything you're associating with each peg an outrageous memory of some sort. You can have fun with this as you're dreaming up ridiculous scenarios to associate with each peg.

Use your imagination to see how you can expand this technique beyond just memorizing groceries. If you're reading a history book, chunk down into chapters and summarize only four main things in each chapter, using the memory palace concept each time. For example, if the Statue of Liberty is one thing you need to remember, imagine her dropping her flame and having to bend over to pick it up. Associated items that are funny actions are easiest to remember.

5) Repeat the journey in your mind.

Now everything you want to remember is firmly planted. All you need to do is conduct another walkthrough, again and again, noticing the silly objects you've planted, all in their respective places.

Remember to always start out your walkthrough in the same place, and always travel each room in the same sequence. As you walk through each room, notice the funny actions you've created and replay them in your mind.

Once you can walk through and remember each event in their respective places successfully, it's time to reverse the walk and to go through your palace from end to start, again paying very close attention to each memory plant associated with each memory peg.

If you're having difficulty at first, make sure you are in a place where you can apply complete focus to this activity.

The great thing about using the memory palace is that it's not only extremely effective, but also FUN! Think again about how Sherlock Holmes puts his thoughts in his "brain attic".

Exercise B

At the grocery store you bought: twelve ears of corn, six bars of soap, three gallons of milk, three bags of cookie dough, twelve bunches of bananas, and four boxes of cereal. Is that correct?

8

MAKING DEDUCTIONS FROM BODY LANGUAGE & DETECTING DECEIT

When making deductions with people, body language is the first clue where you'd want to keep watch. You've seen those episodes with "Sherlock Holmes", "Colombo", "Monk", or even "House": it's the tick, the blush, the hand tremor, the touch on the nose. These all are indications of how to find the perpetrator.

Why Body Language Is Important in Deduction

93% of all communication is nonverbal. Do you believe that? Think about a friend of yours who may have, teasingly, called you an offensive name, but at the same time, smiled or winked at you. Did you take offense? No, of course not, even though the words may have been downright rude or hurtful, you did not take offense. Instead, you laughed. You knew your friend was kidding because the body language told you otherwise. This proves that people pay more attention to body language than simple words.

So How Can You Develop that "Sherlock Holmes Intuition"?

Much of what investigators notice are what others miss. The ability to read nonverbal communication, such as a gestures, will give you a clue as to what conclusions you should reach. Everyone reveals some sort of body language that whispers their innermost thoughts to you. You'll want to take note of body language, and from that, derive much of the data you will need to solve a problem.

According to the body language expert, Allan Pease, there are basically three ways of interpreting body language, remembered as the "three C's": cluster, congruence and context.

Interpreting Gestures in Clusters

Just as a single word can't convey a meaning until you hear the entire sentence. A single gesture also needs to be seen in the context of clusters. Three gestures, similar to three words for a sentence, reveal the entire thought.

Notice Gestures That Are Incongruent in Context

It is a dead giveaway when you see a gesture noting friendliness and, at the same time, you notice hostility. Danger!

For example, suppose a guy is on a date with a girl and his entire body is turned facing her, as if he wants to listen to her. However, his eyes are saying something entirely different. Every time a stranger walks by, his eyes glance toward the stranger and away from the girl. While his words might be saying that he agrees with her, his incongruent gestures are giving away his true inner feelings.

Another example is the famous incongruent smile. The mouth is turned up like a smile should be, but the eyes aren't "smiling" with the wrinkles showing off the feeling.

Once you have the ability to spot a contradiction between what someone is saying and their body language, you have the ability to be perceptive.

Notice Gestures That Are Out of Context

The gesture of crossed arms usually means that the person is shut off and does not want to listen. In fact, studies show people who sit in at seminars with their arms crossed retain 38% less information.

However, people also will cross their arms if they're cold, or they might have a friendly attitude, but just happen to be holding a book in that position. The entire context needs to be taken into account before labeling anyone with a character trait due to their body language.

For example, you might see a man in a seated position carrying on a conversation with someone else. However, he keeps putting his hand up to his mouth. He might be hiding something; he might want to say something; or he could be a smoker.

SIGNS OF DOMINATION

What Sherlock Holmes Did

When a potential client came into his office to present a case to him, Sherlock sat straight up in his chair. Sometimes he crossed his legs. That wasn't a sign of rejection or hiding. The message was: "Maybe I'll take this case on. Maybe I won't. Convince me."

Once he became interested, he leaned forward toward the client —

not too far forward, mind you. It conveyed a message of interest. He acted differently with women. When he leaned forward, he may have bent a little and rested his lower arms on his knee. The purpose of that was to show the woman that he was not a threat or someone who is to be feared. Respected, yes. Intimidating, no.

If someone shakes your hand and their hand is on top, that person is trying to dominate you. The best rapport is generated with an equal handshake with both parties squeezing equal pressure, both on the same angle to the ground. To make sure you're able to create an equal handshake, step to the left and forward a little when approaching a stranger for a handshake. Touching other parts of the body when shaking a stranger's hand is not recommended. However, a brief touch to the elbow of the stranger has been shown to generate good feelings.

If you want to portray a look of confidence when speaking in public or in an interview, a gesture with hands together with fingertips touching is best.

Pointing or making gestures with accenting the points in your discussion with your forefinger and thumb touching helps you to come across as authoritative without looking too aggressive.

Holding hands behind the back displays confidence, while holding hands on the hips with elbows out displays aggression, preparing to dominate. The complete hand inside the pocket indicates aggression, while leaving thumbs out indicates superiority. Male teenagers do that a lot. They are trying to convey to you the fact that they are more competent than their peers, or even that they are "in charge" of the conversation. Cops can usually spot a gang leader when they see that gesture. If the hands are held out from the body, this also shows that they are feeling superior.

Men who sit with open and uncrossed legs are showing dominance as the "alpha male". The "legs-open" gesture is actually true about dominance, whether sitting or standing.

When a person sits inappropriately in a chair (as some children or adolescents do), they're showing you that they don't see you as important and they feel they are dominant. Police interrogators frequently note this and watch closely as the questioning proceeds. And, if someone faces you with a chair in front of them with the back facing you, it's a strong indication of dominance and stubbornness.

SIGNS OF MISTRUST

A person will fold their hands in front of the body when they don't trust you. Additionally, if the biceps are grasped at the same time, this demonstrates insecurity.

There are several different ways to interpret arms crossing, however. Arms crossed with fists forming will indicate hostility, while arms crossed with thumbs up shows that they're warming up to you.

Women sometimes use their purse to "shield" them from you if they feel threatened. Dentists notice this and treat those women very gently. During the treatment, they will often say: "Raise your finger if this hurts."

Also, be aware of a person with a drink who puts the drink on the opposite side from which they're drinking; that shows mistrust as well.

If a person has both of their legs and arms crossed when sitting, never ask them to make a decision. They don't trust you. Furthermore, if they're holding their crossed leg with their hands, it's a sign of stubbornness.

LIE DETECTION

Trying to detect whether or not a person is lying is difficult. The best setting is a simple one — something like a table that is open on the bottom, a couple of chairs, a couple of water bottles, a glass, a couple of notepads, and a few pens. Situate your own chair slightly away from the table so you can observe the person's legs.

You want to see the lower portion of the body because that is more honest than the torso. Signs of discomfort will especially be revealed by the position of the legs.

Liars will sometimes place objects between you and themselves. For example, a water bottle, glass, notepad, pens, etc. That means the person you are questioning wants to conceal something. Perhaps the person is leaning back with the lower legs bent so as to be under the chair. Liars seldom touch you in any way. They will not touch your hands. If someone is touching your hand and suddenly pulls away, then take their forthcoming statement with a grain of salt.

Remember, though, that all of those behaviors may or may not mean deception. You need to judge that by the entire impression you derive from the person's body and the content of their speech.

Lying can be detected more easily in children, as they haven't yet learned how to control the giveaway signs. But strangely enough, people have a tendency to make a gesture from hand to face as if to block information.

Examples of a more repressed version like you would see in adults would be a nose rub, tug on the ear or touching the eyebrows to indicate deceit. People who are introduced to something they don't want to see are likely to rub their eyes or blink a lot. It's a powerful display of disagreement.

FACIAL EXPRESSIONS

A frown, a grimace, and glancing to the person's left may indicate deception. Any expression that lasts too long to be considered normal indicates that the person is deliberately trying to pretend he is experiencing an emotion. For example, if the person has a frozen smile on his face. If a person lets out a little laugh when you confront or contradict him or her, that is a sign of extreme discomfort. A continual smile when everyone else is serious can come off as creepy or fake. News commentators on a panel frequently do this. It often means that the opposing argument is the better one. Fidgeting is anxiety, of course. "Eye blocking" by means of rubbing the eyes or holding the palms over the eyes or even closing the eyes shows extreme discomfort and may be evidence of deceit. A flutter of the eyelids is also seen when a person is extremely uncomfortable. A false smile usually appears stronger on one side versus the other, and a tight lip smile where teeth are not shown shows that the person is trying to keep a secret.

Any sudden change in a person's expressions generally indicates deceit.

THE EYES TELL ALL

The human eye, often called the "window to the soul", tells many tales. Many people are taught that good eye contact is important for communication. However, the research shows that it's best to look someone square in the eye only about 50% of the time. Too much is staring, and too little is not caring. Allan Pease advises that you should actually give the other person at least three seconds to look you over before speaking or engaging in conversation with a new stranger. This is suggested to establish an initial trust with a stranger. In establishing rapport with a new person, eye contact should be maintained about 60–70% of the time until you are finished with the introductory phase.

The following characteristics of eyes tell even more:

- Eyes constricted means that the person is not open or in agreeance with what they're hearing. That is not a good time to try to land them on your call to action. Conversely, dilated eyes (enlarged pupils) reveal openness and trust, and can also indicate a problem-solving mode. If you're trying to sell someone on an idea and their eyes are dilated, it's time for your call to action! More than likely, their decision will be positive. If you're in a conversation, notice the eye dilation; they're interested in you if pupils are dilated, and they're challenging you if the pupils are constricted.

- Eyes looking to the right and up indicate the person is trying to remember something they know. Eyes straight across to the right would reflect auditory memory, and up to the right reflect visual memory. However, looking up and to the left indicates an attempt to try to make something up, and down to the left indicates making up something with feeling.

  You can actually try this out on yourself. Try to remember what you wore yesterday and notice what happens with your eyes. Now try to picture what your kitchen would look like with polka-dotted wallpaper. Notice your eyes glancing toward the left?

- Eyes looking down to the left are a sign of sensory memory, a memory of feeling or emotion. If you're trying to envision what it would be like to wake up in a bed of roses, your eyes look down and to the left. Eyes looking down and to the right indicate inner conversation with one's self. This is also a possible tell-tale of deceit as someone might be trying to create a memory that isn't real.

- The gesture of eyes darting in several directions is a sign of insecurity. This tells you that person is not really enjoying conversation with you, and perhaps you need to help them feel more secure.

Looking down rather than straight into your eyes is not necessarily a sign of deceit. It could be self-consciousness. However, if a person suddenly looks at you straight in the eyes and that is different from their prior expressions, it may very well be a lie. Killers will **lock** their eyes on you and say: "I didn't kill that woman!"

HEAD MOVEMENTS

If someone moves as they are speaking, this is normal. It is usually considered to be a sign of truthfulness. However, if the movement comes *after* the person has spoken, it is fake.

Sometimes people make statements in the affirmative, but their heads are shaking "No". Take note of this. Head movements in the affirmative should match affirmative statements, and vice versa. When you watch an interview on TV with an official or politician, you will often notice a mismatch of the head movement and their statements. Politicians are especially prone to this. If you are astute, it will leave you with a sense of ambiguity.

SUBTLE MANIFESTATIONS

You would need some practice to notice subtleties. People who are uncomfortable may become slightly ruddy in complexion and they may sweat just a bit. That is not terribly noticeable unless you have educated yourself to look closely. Like facial flushes, paleness or loss of skin tone is a sign of fear. Bodily trembling, of course, shows nervousness, but a deliberate attempt to control bodily movements like clasping the hands together to keep them from fidgeting, forcefully holding the arms down so they don't swing about, and the like are signs of deception. Compressed lips are a very significant sign of deception.

If someone swallows a lot, or clears his or her throat frequently it is more a sign of anxiety than deception. However, if a person's speech patterns become inconsistent with the patterns you heard earlier in the interview, it may very well be a sign of unmitigated deceit.

PACIFIERS

Women will tend to play with their hair when they are trying to calm themselves down. Sometimes, men with very light beards — as is common today in the West — will rub their whiskers. This, too, is pacifying behavior. People may also "pet" themselves, by gently rubbing one palm on top of their other hand. If you notice this behavior, it could be that the issue you are addressing is problematic for them. It is a sign of distress that may indicate deceit.

PSYCHOTICS AND SOCIOPATHS

People who are psychopaths or sociopaths love to talk about themselves, for the most part. Psychopaths fantasize a lot, so it is difficult to separate fact from fiction. Sociopaths are extremely manipulative and clever. They will tell you what they think you want to hear. If they are very good at it, you will end up liking them. Ted Bundy, for example, was quite charming. However, if you compare some of his video interviews, you would notice that he said one thing to one interviewer, and something entirely different to another. Sociopaths are skillful liars.

Paranoid schizophrenics are much more reluctant to talk — for obvious reasons. Other types of schizophrenics are generally aware of their illness and it makes them very self-conscious. They are afraid of lapsing into bizarre behavior.

9

HOW TO IMPROVE YOUR
DEDUCTIVE & INDUCTIVE SKILLS

CRITICAL THINKING

When examining all data to start making deductions, it is imperative that you keep all emotions out of the way and use critical thinking.

Critical thinking refers to thinking logically and objectively when analyzing or evaluating an issue. It takes practice to look at all angles objectively and without judgement. But this kind of thinking is necessary for investigators to make the right choices, or for you to make the right decision in your life. The quality of your thinking can be systematically cultivated to help you make better decisions. Critical thinking is self-disciplined and self-monitored, as there is a constant strive for improvement.

As a qualified critical thinker, you should:

- Identify important questions concerning the issue and state the questions clearly.
- Assemble all data and assess pertinent information, using complex understanding.
- Arrive at a well-thought-out conclusion. But it doesn't stop there. Now you need to test your conclusion objectively against other relevant criteria.

- Think objectively, with an open mind towards any or all possibilities.
- Communicate your findings with others to mastermind for better possible solutions.

Remember, it's the thinking that you've done so far in your life that has brought you to where you are now. Quality of thought equals qualify of life. It's as simple as that. Try the following exercises first and then re-evaluate your thinking style in light of the information that follow.

Exercise A	
Read the following:	Did you notice an ambiguity in that passage?
Mr. Zazzara was quite furious. His wife told him that their daughter, who was working for a bank, was embezzling money, but it was being done so cleverly that she would not be detected. Mr. and Mrs. Zazzara were rather poor. Mrs. Zazzara said that the money would certainly come in handy. However, Mr. Zazzara was a very honest man and wanted to insist that his daughter stop it. He and his wife argued about it a lot. With his daughter being an embezzler and his wife miserable, one evening after making his decision, the girl's father called her into his study and said…	What was it? _____ _____ _____ _____ _____ How would you get clarification on it? _____ _____ What do you think the father said? _____

Exercise B

Read the following and determine if the inferences are valid or not.

1. Most politicians are dishonest. After all, most ordinary people are dishonest – and politicians are ordinary people.

2. It will rain today. The rain clouds show up clearly on the weather satellite, and are headed this way.

3. Philip is taller than Sue; and Sarah is shorter than Sue. So Philip is taller than Sarah.

4. At four, Mike is always either at the café or in the library. Whenever Mike is in the library, he's sucking on a lozenge. Mike was not in the café when I looked at four, so he was in the library.

5. No experienced accountant is incompetent. Ferguson always makes mistakes. No competent accountant always makes mistakes. Therefore, Ferguson is inexperienced.

6. Many city officials take kickbacks. Most city officials have extra-marital affairs. So many people who take kickbacks have extra-marital affairs.

7. Many people are over six feet tall. Few women are over six feet tall. So, few, if any people are women.

8. If Herbert is a horse, he isn't human; so if Herbert isn't human, he is a horse.

Analyze Your Personal Choices and Refine
Your Thinking Technique for the Future

Reflect on your own personal experience and the choices you've made in your lifetime. Most likely, you have not arrived at your life choices objectively. As you recall your major life choice, answer the follow questions:

1) What choice did I have to make and what was the situation?
2) What alternatives did I have at the time for which I was not aware?
3) Did I miss those alternatives?
4) Why did I miss possible alternate life choices?
5) If I had considered all the other pertinent choices, how would I have acted?

It's easy for us to blame the problems we have on someone else, claiming that there was really no alternate road. However, this only brings you back to square one in the end. It's the very reason that the wives of abusers remarry to another man similar to the one she left. It's the reason why you can't seem to find that job or career that you really enjoy. It's even the reason why diets don't work.

Once you can accept responsibility for your own actions, you now have the ability to move forward to make better life choices and better decisions, and hence, shaping a new and improved life.

As a logical thinker, you need to develop the skill of diagnosing problems for customers or clients. Whether you're looking for ways to better evaluate what bills need paying, or ways to fix a computer, sharpening your critical thinking tools can always help.

PRACTICAL TIPS FOR PUTTING AN EDGE ON YOUR CRITICAL THINKING

The Conditional Statement

Think about a cause and effect, and state it clearly. For example, you could say, "If it rains, then then school is cancelled."

Let's take that sentence and dissect it. The first half "If it rains" is conditional. A logical statement with cause and effect is a conditional statement. The second part of the sentence, "then school is cancelled" is the result of the condition. This is logic — if the first part of the sentence is fulfilled, the latter will be true.

Conditional statements are worked a lot with math problems, but this kind of logical thinking can be applied to any situation. The conditional part of the sentence is the premise, and the second part of the sentence is the conclusion. Sometimes you see these in shorthand, as "p" and "q".

Even though the statement about taking care of the environment doesn't relate to math, the premise/conclusion shorthand can still be applied. If "p" then "q", then it is represented as follows, "p → q".

The Converse, Inverse, and Contrapositive

Now that you understand p and q, it's easier to understand the converse, inverse, and contrapositive with logical thinking.

What Is A "Converse Statement"?

This is where the premise and conclusion are reversed. An example of a converse statement would be "If school is cancelled, then it must have rained".

But, wait a minute… does that mean that *any time* school is cancelled it's because of rain? Of course not! This means that the converse statement is a false syllogism.

The converse statement is not true because there are several different reasons why school could be cancelled apart from a rainy day.

Does the following make any sense?

- It is rains, then school is cancelled.
- School was cancelled.
- Therefore, it must have rained.

Another false syllogism is as follows:

- Cows have four legs.
- Horses have four legs.
- Therefore, cows are horses.

What Is an Inverse Statement?

With an inverse statement, the premise and conclusion stay in the same place in the sentence, but both premise and conclusion are negated.

Let's take a look at the school inverse statement:

"If it *does not* rain, then school *is not* cancelled."

Here again, the reverse does not make any sense.

What Is the Contrapositive Statement?

This switches the premise and conclusion, and negates both.

"If school is not cancelled, then it has not rained." If the original statement is true, then the contrapositive statement is the only statement that should also be true in every case. In this illustration, the contrapositive statement does not make sense. Therefore, you can't draw the conclusion that your original statement is true.

CRITICAL THINKING VS. INTUITION

Logical and critical thinking might be helpful with simple life choices – like finding your keys.

"When I lose my keys, I always find them in the last place I had them."

The contrapositive of that is: "If I don't find my keys in the last place I had them, then I didn't lose my keys." Knowing that the above statement is true can help you remember to think about where you were instead of doing stupid things like looking under the bed.

10

HOW TO IMPROVE YOUR DECISION-MAKING ABILITY THROUGH DEDUCTION

Why Do People Make Bad Decisions?

It's difficult to think objectively when emotions get in the way. That's why step five of the critical thinking steps noted above is "communicate your findings with others". Remember how Holmes would express his findings to Watson? That's what your friends are for.

> *"In leadership, it's important to be*
> *intuitive, but not at the expense of facts."*
> *-Michel Dell, founder of Dell Computers*

If only there were someone who would tell you the formula for what you should do all the time, you wouldn't have to worry about making bad decisions. Well, as it turns out, someone did. In the 1738, Daniel Bernoulli, a Dutch mathematician, has a "formula" for this:

> *"The expected value of any of our actions —*
> *that is, the goodness that we can count*
> *on getting — is the product of two simple*
> *things: the odds that this action will allow*
> *us to gain something, and the value of that*

gain to us.”
-Daniel Bernoulli

Sounds simple on the surface; if you can estimate and multiply these two items, you can always anticipate the outcome.

The problem is that rational decisions *do not* always aim to gain maximum health and happiness. The more you reject, the more loss you feel. Unfortunately, there's always human error involved. People make errors in estimating the gain that they will feel, and they also make errors in estimating the value of the success.

Calculating Odds for Estimating Gain

People tend to calculate in general by scanning their memories for past situations, and come up with a quick conclusion. If you were asked if it's more common to see dogs on leashes or cats on leashes, you would very quickly reply "dogs, of course". So this is a really a useful rule of thumb.

Except It Doesn't Always Work!

Suppose you were asked whether there are more 4-letter words in the English language with the first letter R or the third letter R. The mind recalls words that begin with R first, even though, in reality, there are more words with the letter R in the third place. This is an example of how the mind can lead you astray.

People tend to make decisions on things because they make a quick "scan" in their brains. People think about situations to which they have been exposed and make that "quick brain scan" decision.

This can be dangerous if you're not aware of why you're making that decision.

For example, why do people play the lottery?

Statistics tell people that they're more likely to get struck by lightning than win the lottery, so why do they play?

Marketing has a lot to do with why folks make stupid choices. They scan their brains and think about that nice couple they heard on the radio who won five million dollars. They remember the winners they've seen on TV. And, in a short period of time, they buy that ticket, and think about the possibilities of becoming rich. The hormone, serotonin, is released in their brains and they feel happy. That feeling outweighs the feeling they get when they discover they didn't win. In truth, they never really expected to win in the first place.

ERRORS IN VALUE

Additionally, people tend to make those "quick brain scan" comparisons when estimating value.

Would you pay $20 for a bottle of water? Of course not. Your brain compares what you know to the value of the water, and you know that water isn't worth that much. But what if you were crossing the desert on foot and there was no way you could buy any water? Suddenly the water becomes more valuable. Rather than comparing the investment to other possible investments, you made the choice "it's not worth that much" based on your past experience.

Making decisions based on past experience can befuddle the decisions you make, because you fail to see the entire context.

People Make Choices Based on Comparison

Marketers love this! You see things that are "marked down" in the store all the time – and are you more likely to buy? Of course!

You might see a wine from $20 to $15, so you believe at the time what you're buying is a great deal. However, once you get home, you really can't tell the difference between that new bottle and the $10 bottle in your refrigerator.

You have just been duped by a marketing scam that made you believe you were getting a good deal when you weren't. This is because you didn't look at the entire situation in context.

Another Value Judgement Error

You need a new car stereo, and the cost at the dealer in your neighborhood is $200. But you have an offer to get the same stereo for only $100 on the other side of town. Do you drive across town to save $100? Most people would.

Now suppose you were buying a new car with a stereo and the cost was $40,000, but if you drove across town, you would get the car for $39,900. Would you drive across town to another dealership to save that $100? Most people would not.

We tend to not take things into the proper context.

Errors in Judgement and Time

The problem with decision making when making comparisons is even more difficult when the choices are arrayed over time.

Basically, there are two reasons why people make bad decisions over time: they tend to rationalize the following:

1) More is always better than less.
2) Now is always better than later.

So, you find yourself paying high interest rates to have your cake NOW, rather than later.

What's interesting is that people can make the impatience go away by simply changing the expected time of gratification.

Would you rather get $50 in a year or $60 in 13 months? Most people tell themselves, "I'm already waiting a year, what's one more month?" And they elect the latter. Yet if you were given the same opportunity to get $50 now or $60 next month, you'll probably want to take $50 *NOW*.

When you look into the distance, your perception is more correct then when you look at something with the expectation of receiving it now.

> *"What space is to size; time is to value"*
> *-Plato*

When people get into the future, they change their minds.

This is why people underestimate the odds of their future pain and overestimate the value of their future pleasure.

YOUR NEW POSITIVE LIFE DECISION

Now you're aware that knowing what you want and deciding to go after it is everything. You're cognizant of the fact that writing down your decision brings forth the desire to take action. It is action that will turn your dreams into reality.

You're now aware that whenever you ask yourself a stupid question, you can give yourself a better question in order to get a better answer. Now you know that better answers can always be provided for you when you ask with positive expectations.

You trust your intuition now, because you're more confident that whatever happens is fine with you.

Perhaps the formula given by Daniel Bernoulli would have worked if peoples' brains didn't have to combat the issues given them in today's world. The human brain evolved in a world in which the highest priority is to eat and mate, and have little contact with anyone outside of one's own culture.

This punctuates the issue of how important it is for you to start re-training your brain to think more critically and start looking at the decisions you make in full context of the situation at hand.

The *only thing* that can destroy you is making a bad decision.

CONCLUSION

It only remains now to say that detection is essential for coming across as a more intelligent and knowledgeable person. The results are immensely rewarding. You have learned how to develop and engage your powers of observation to discern, not just to "see". You will be able to make more informed choices in your life, and transform yourself into that person who lurks within you. It is said that people use only a fraction of their minds. With the information above, you are now equipped to create new neural pathways in your brain and reformulate your thinking in such a way that it truly serves you. If you deliberately practice these techniques, your IQ score would actually increase. Although it is said that IQ's do not change, all IQ tests have a standard deviation. That means that you can deviate from your original score by a set number of points. You have learned how to revitalize your powers of creativity and innovation in order to derive a new set of behaviors. There is chapter devoted to reading body language. That has given you the ability to detect deceit and the skills necessary in order to "listen" to the unspoken communications of others.

ABOUT THE AUTHOR

Stefan Cain has spent the majority of his working career in numerous academic research positions, working on a wealth of psychological, societal and cultural topics. His research work and adept studies have been used to form the backbone of many popular titles available today, providing him with the experience and hunger to delve deeper into some avenues of thought.

Alongside his serious academic work, Stefan has been published in a number of prominent publications; filing news reports, features and insightful opinion pieces on myriad topics throughout his career. It was here, in this capacity as a journalist, that he first began to start writing about human behavior.